Speak Life

Sherika V. Washington

PublishAmerica
Baltimore

© 2005 by Sherika V. Washington.
All rights reserved. No part of this book may be reproduced, stored in a retrieval system or transmitted in any form or by any means without the prior written permission of the publishers, except by a reviewer who may quote brief passages in a review to be printed in a newspaper, magazine or journal.

First printing

At the specific preference of the author, PublishAmerica allowed this work to remain exactly as the author intended, verbatim, without editorial input.

ISBN: 1-4137-9723-7
PUBLISHED BY PUBLISHAMERICA, LLLP
www.publishamerica.com
Baltimore

Printed in the United States of America

Speak Life

Sherika V. Washington

Foreword by:
Bishop Joseph D. McBride

To my husband, Robert and our children, Anthony, Treasure, and Jaylin.

Thank you for speaking my dream into existence long before it was alive in me.

*To my parents,
Curtis and Marie Martin.*

All of your love, support, and hard work have not been in vain. I love you and I appreciate all you've done for me.

SPECIAL DEDICATION

To the late Timica Bradley (Johnson)
my best friend since high school.
You've gone on to a better place.
Sooner than I thought but I guess you finished your race.
Just wanted you to know our dream is coming true.
My first book has been published and I dedicate it to you.

Acknowledgments

I'd like to thank my pastor, Bishop Joseph D. McBride. It is through your teaching, guidance and obedience to God that I am able to take this step. Thank you for taking the time to prepare the foreword for this book and for your support.

To his wife, my spiritual mother, Elder Jerlean McBride, thank you for being the strong woman of God that you are. You are my example, inspiration, and proof that I too can be a virtuous woman of God .

To my big sisters (who are smaller than me) thank you. Thanks for supporting me and believing in my dream. Your willingness to help pushed me to work harder. The way you made yourselves available to me made me believe I could accomplish anything. You are the best big sisters a baby girl could ever have. I love you.

To Tamara Ester. Girl it is finally happening. Thanks for your support and congratulations on "All in the Name of Love" a great novel and best wishes on its success. I'm waiting for novel #2.

Special Thanks to everyone who purchased this book. I pray it blesses your soul and strengthens and encourages you.

Contents

Foreword	13
Special Presentation	14
Introduction	15
I Am Who I Am	**19**
Sense and Self and Sense	21
Expression	22
Back In the Fire	23
Words to the Wise	24
A Holy Presentation	25
The Wonder Years	26
See Saw View	27
Running Scared	28
Preferably	29
I Am	30
A Treasure of My Own	31
I Wash'em	32
Dear Treasure	33
Chosen Way	34
My Temple Needs a Turnaround	35
Sometimes We Cry	**37**
Who Am I?	39
My Purpose	40
From Here	41
I Will Prosper	42
Other Times We Fight Back	**43**
Untitled	45
Help is Enough	46
Enough Help	47

I'm So Happy	48
Coming of Age	49
As a Matter of Fact or Cut Like That	
	50
Avoid the Chore	51
A Word to the Wise	52

Occasionally We Drift Away — 53
Blind Journey	54
Spotlight	55

Through It All We Must Speak Life
	57
The Real Thing	59
Too Many Teachings	60
Anna Carson—The Seeker	61
Ms. Melanie—The One who Sows	62
Doubt and Reason	63
Get Busy	64
Make It Work	65

Who are you? — 66
Love Anew	67
Keep the Faith	68
Looking Upon	69
Ponder Life	70
Never Alone	71
The Little Things	72
Sunset Rivers	73
In Prayer	74
Fire and Desire	75
Create a Praise	76
Hearts of Gold	78
Talent Breathes Deeply	79
Thank You	80
More than Thank You	81
One Moment	82

Foreword

Although each poem is a tidbit of her personal life, the writings of Sister Sherika cause you to delve deeply into your spirit as you seek to hear from God.

There is nothing more intimate than to hear that still quiet voice that gives you the assurance that God is talking directly to you.

As you read each poem, you are able to feel the spiritual tug of our Lord Jesus as He not only portrays that He is Lord of all, but the Lord of your soul.

Read with confidence, read with openness as conflict, pain, joy, and peace cause you to understand that through each phase of natural life on earth, your spiritual life in God becomes your rock, the very foundation from which you're able to stand each test.

Bishop Joseph D. McBride,
Pastor/Overseer Praise & Deliverance Temple Ministries
Jenkinsville, SC

God doesn't do anything by accident. He sends his flock to the shepherd who will effectively lead them back home to the Father. He has equipped each shepherd with exactly what they need in order to relate to and understand their followers. I am a writer and because God foreknew this day would come He sent me to a Bishop who would not only support me but one who shares the same gift.

It is an honor for me to offer a "special presentation" of one of the many gifts God placed inside: Bishop Joseph McBride.

Father We Give Thee Thanks

For each beautiful, bountiful gift you send,
For every kind and loyal friend,
For quickly supplying every need,
For keeping my mind from thoughts of greed,
For this gift of health along the way,
As you keep me strong day to day,

For helping hands and a voice of cheer,
For ears that listen; your voice to hear,
For tongue filled laughter, and a voice to talk,
For ordered steps, Your path to walk,
For spiritual eyes Your Word I read,
For your commands I strive to heed,
Father I give thanks to Thee,
For without You, where would I be!

Christmas Time Is Here Again

Christmas time is here again,
And thoughts of Christ bring joy within.
Because God gave His only Son,
To redeem mankind from the evil one.
Some will party and forget
That He came for them, this they'll regret.
But eternity it will remind
Them of the Christ they left behind
Let us who love Him not forget,
Why Jesus came, His fate was set.
He came to set the captives free,
He came for you, He came for me
Oh what joy this Gift does bring,
And of His praises I will sing.
Such joy He brings I feel within
At Christmas time here once again.

Introduction

This collection of poems will open the door to a movement. I feel a shift in the atmosphere and it is going to be controlled by what we speak out of our mouths. I selected these poems to present myself to you. Within these pages is my captured heart. I'm filled with love, encouragement, and positivism. Nevertheless, I am far from delusional. I realize the seriousness of the times and more than a few sweet verses are required for battle. Fear not I am battletested and prepared.

My website, justspeaklife.zoomshare.com gives the heart of the movement. I have a plan to speak to everyone who will listen (and some who won't) about the power of what we say. "Speak Life" is going to be followed by "The Lecture." In the next book I will address speaking life, the how, why, when, and what it's all about.

These poems introduce my straightforward approach and my passion. This passion causes me to feel a twinge when I hear a mother curse her child. I cry inside when three criminals in a row on the evening news are of color. I feel the frustration of parents who are doing their best to no apparent avail.

I want to share a concept with the world that will change lives for generations to come. As you read these poems allow the words to fill your heart and breathe life into every dead situation you may be facing.

May God Bless You!!!

I.

I Am Who I Am...

I am falling in love with who I am becoming. Every day I can say I love myself. It hasn't always been this way but I thank God that it is now.

    I experienced the "low self esteem issues". I hated myself for not being light-skinned and not having long hair. I despised my parents for not being rich (even though I got EVERYTHING I wanted). I guess it was because my Dad was a carpenter, not a lawyer and my Mom was a C.N.A. and not an RN. It never donned on me that my Dad was the lead man and my Mom became a supervisor. To think, they loved me any way.

    I experienced life early and made many mistakes. I often regret it but I realize now what part those mistakes played in the drama that is my life. I look back and realize there are only a few things about my past that I would change and those wounds have been healed through my poetry.

    I've grown from footloose and fancy free on the inside and wise beyond my years on the outside, to saved on the inside and wild on the outside and vice-versa depending on my surroundings, to saved inside and out regardless of my surroundings. It's been a long time coming and it will be a long time going but I'll enjoy it all the way. After all, I am who I am.

Sense and Self and Sense

What sense does it make to talk
to someone who's not sensible?
What reason is there to talk to someone who's not reasonable?
Why write a poem no one will read?
Simply, to express myself and help relieve me.

Expression is breadth in my body!

My right hand is my heart and as it draws the words on the page I live. Its like I'm suffocating and the pen's movement gives me air. And the final sentence is the deep sigh of relief.

Back In the Fire

I stepped in the fire again and
Your grace kept me from getting burned.
What have I done to deserve
all the mercy and grace I've earned?
I wish I could make a list, maybe I'd feel better about myself
Instead I'll begin to thank you for all my strength and health.
I don't feel too saved right now because yes, I've sinned again
But thanks for getting me home safely
through the stormy rains.
It's not hard for me to acknowledge all that You do for me
My struggles come in all that I try to do, you see.
Pleasing my flesh and all those worldly needs
I ask humbly again that you forgive me once more please?

Close Encounter

Have you ever been so full
you thought you were going to burst?
When that fire on the inside makes moving a must.
Yesterday I felt that in my arms and in my legs
By God's Spirit I was being fed.
I was filled to the top and pouring over the sides
None of this feeling did I try to hide.
I was in a place, just me and God
I'm sure to those standing by I looked pretty odd.
But my Daddy talked to me, comforted me and loved on me.
This was going on and no one could see.
I was blessed and today is my test
Satan is definitely going to give me his best.
But his best can't stand against my Father's mighty hand
So I'll move out of the way and let God spoil his plan.

A Holy Presentation

The gates of the dungeon are open and
I am about to walk out.
This is a day I've longed for and repeatedly dreamed about.
No more bondage, that is far from me
No more endless tears hindering my ability to see.
No longer serving a master half-heartedly and expecting fair
and gentle treatment.
Instead, serving my only Master with a faithful commitment.
The heat that awaits me on the other side of those gates
Presents the cool of the dungeon as a good place to wait.
But I've been released and there's favor in my life
I'm trusting God to make every wrong right.
Once the dungeon is warmer and the gatekeeper changed,
I'll be presented as a vessel, holy and unashamed.

The Wonder Years

Critters crawling
Hair falling
Foul odor and moisture to boot.
Peers teasing, laughing, and saying that's a hoot.
Shots or pills maybe both
Spots or bumps or an abnormal growth.
Many endured and eventually healed.
I praise God that your grace and mercy never did yield
And thank You for the wonder years.

See Saw View

The heat had risen many times before
But this time I knew the moment of truth
was knocking at my door.
Answering was not a question,
I had wanted this so bad for so long.
In fact I found myself helping to move things along.
So there I was out in the open for all the world to see
Sitting there, bare with nothing or no one protecting me.
How was I blessed and perfectly kept?
I was escorted home and not simply left.
I came out of it alone, as one and not two.
I look back and to my Father in heaven say thank you.

Running Scared

My flesh moves in my sleep and I awaken down by three
I glance into the mirror and there I see an image of me.
Godly with ungodly thoughts
The righteousness of God doing wrong.
Some days I walk away humming the words to a love song
Others I leave getting my praise on.
Am I straddling the fence?
No, I love God with all my heart
I think I'm running scared because my destiny is about to start.
I titled this running scared and that's how I'm writing right now.
My destiny is about to come to pass and I couldn't stop it even if I knew how.
I must simply study to show myself approved
And make myself a holy vessel, willing to be used.

Preferably

It's not that I can't weather a storm
I just prefer to stay dry.
I've been thrust into situations beyond my control
Yet I endured the pain most times alone.
I've been given people and some taken away
But I always managed to last to see a brighter day.
I've been hurt in places I didn't know I had
I've smiled beautiful smiles though my heart was sad.
I know I can weather any storm,
I simply prefer to stay dry.

I Am

I am proud of who I am
I believe in what is right
I come from a long line of geniuses
and I am willing to fight!
Fight for freedom and for justice for myself and others,
I respect all of creation because all in creation are my brothers.
I am beautiful just as I am
Smart and talented, too.
I appreciate myself and I appreciate you!

A Treasure of My Own

She moved the big tiger in position to raise my feet.
Despite all my fussing and ordering
she's there for my needs to meet.
She's the angel God has given me to care for me
when I am weak.
To render a smile or hug or touch ever so meek.
I love my Treasure whom God has blessed.
Through her I'll give Him nothing less than my best.

I Wash'em

I wash the dishes to no avail
Each time I wash them they're used again.
Nevertheless, I wash them clean, spotless each time
Not a speck of food will be on any dish of mine.
Although it's tiresome and never-ending it seems
I wash those dishes daily until they're squeaky-clean.
This is not because I'm crazy or psychotically obsessed
But because my family deserves only the best.

Dear Treasure

You're my motivation to do better than I am
To take chances, to venture out
and for necessary cause to stand.
You make me want to look my best
And serve God even better than that.
You inspire me to strive for higher heights
Just because of the success I want in your life.
In your eyes I see potential waiting to be developed
In my heart I hold each gaze, enveloped.
Reminding me of why I try when others give up.
Assuring me it's by God's miracles that I am and not luck.
Thank you daughter for being you.
Thank you, because your inspiration is true.

Chosen Way

A lot's been going on in my life.
Started being a businesswoman stopped being a wife.
Uneasy abut both. I know very little about either.
Destined to be a success
Operating like an eager beaver.
Life's experiences are deep
Wisdom and knowledge don't come cheap.
I'm making my way, led by God.
And if the truth is told some of my days are very hard.
Hard is another story for a different day.
This is just to mention my chosen way.

My Temple Needs a Turnaround

My temple has been used, abused and lacked proper rest.
It's been loved, adored and envied no less.
Never mind the world's damage; I've done enough on my own.
From drinking and sex to no self-love and hate of my skin tone.
My temple is now fifty pounds broader than I want it to be
Not because of what the world says but because of me.
I don't like to jiggle and shake when I walk
I don't want two or three chins to appear when I talk.
I want to wrestle with my children and not fear breaking their bones.
I want to love myself when I'm all-alone.
There was a time when the mirror was a friend of mine.
Not anymore because whenever I see her, my reflection shows up and breaks me down.
I feel beautiful inside and I work hard to maintain my goals of inner-beauty.
But that's not enough
I want to feel as beautiful in the physical me.
Not that the outer beauty isn't there, just not at my goal
And it's important to me that my outer beauty matches my soul.
Judge me all you want, you'll be judged by the same measure.
But satisfying me is my personal pleasure.
Unfortunately, it may cause me to be healthy and thin
Thank goodness for me neither is a sin.

II.

Sometimes we cry and complain...

Nothing in life is perfect. We all know that, but there are some rewards that come pretty close. Unfortunately, to get to those rewards we have to endure some circumstances that don't feel good.

Your question may be how do we speak life in the midst of pain and turmoil. The answer is simple but you must follow me on this. When you are in a bad situation it's okay to complain, get angry and even express your anger. The key is to express all of those emotions to God and not your fellowman. Why? Well, God is the only One who can fix or change your situation. If you take it to your friends you tend to get on one accord and speak more power into the bad situation. Please understand, you do have to be respectful to God, remember He doesn't just control your situation He controls your life. So express your feelings about your situation to God and BE REAL. When you talk to your friends you can speak with confidence about your circumstance being taken care of because now it is truly in God's hands.

Remember God in all that you do because although sometimes we cry and complain He will always be the only One who can fix it for you.

Who Am I?

Quiet hidden by loud laughs and plenty to say.
Staying power in the blocks ready to run away.
Nurturing and loving, supportive and sincere.
Selfish and conniving plotting revenge severe.
Hurt, disgusted and at my wits end.
Sadly, doubtful my heart's tears will ever mend.
Wanting, hoping, desiring, praying.
Trusting in God and standing on what He is saying.
Growing in faith despite occasional falls.
Afraid rapid growth will reveal visions over the walls.
Powerful enough to pull down strongholds
A stronghold myself too stubborn to fold.
Downright scared to move forward or back
Smothering in my standing still with feelings of being slack.
I'm trying, I'm crying, inside I'm dying
I need to know who I am.

My Purpose

Why am I here I often wonder?
Why was I given to my father and mother?
Surely not to work, pay bills, taxes and die.
Hopefully not to laugh, then hurt and eventually cry.
Why am I here, what is my purpose?
Not sure yet but I won't lose focus.
I don't have the answer but I know Who does
So I keep my eyes on what is to come and not on what was.

From Here

I once was a dreamer but all the good ones have faded
My reality overpowered me
and my fantasies were suffocated.
I hold on to the remnants,
which seem to slide through my fingers.
Where are my optimism, my hope and my creativity?
Lost in what I thought was a good idea
Now it's perverted, distorted, and totally unclear.
One question breathes within my chest
Growing from the fertilizer, which is my depth.
Father, where do I go from here?

I Will Prosper

When I look in the mirror I know I shouldn't be here.
I always say I'll change things; this is my year.
But nevertheless, year-to-year, I remain right where I am
Whether I go at it freestyle or with a well thought plan.
So why is this year different?
Why is this the year I'll prosper?
Because this is the year I'll stand on the Gospel.
Not in general, but Word by Word.
I'm gonna stand with a faith most men have never heard.
So I declare I'll prosper in every area of my life
Despite pandemonium, chaos and strife.
I declare I will prosper.

III.

Other times we fight back...

If we are marching in the whole armor of God surely we are not wimps. We are built to stand strong and not be taken advantage of. So there are times when we must stand firm. As long as we do it in a godly manner (not just polite but in accordance with God's Word) there are times when we must fight back.

Untitled

I'm very talkative I can't deny
But to be disregarded makes me want to cry.
To be ignored makes me insane
And makes me eager to inflict pain.
True all I say may not be of interest
But I don't deserve to be disrespected.
If my conversation is a bore
Just don't come around anymore.
That would solve all issues no questions asked.
And your disregard for me and my contempt of you will be a thing of the past.

Help is Enough~Get your act together

Enough implies no more is needed
Enough declares no more begging and pleading.
Enough means nothing more is required
Enough means that all else can be retired.
Enough is enough is enough is enough
We've all heard it before.
Somehow you seemed to have missed the point
so here it is once more.
I've given you what you asked for: help.
I've offered you what you needed: help.
However, "I need more" you continue to yelp.
Well I've supplied enough help and
Help is Enough!
Get Your Act Together!

Enough Help

Called upon to do so much
Depended on to add a touch
Expected to fully deliver
On time, every time, but smiles are clever.
The smile takes away the inconvenience so they think
The smile eases the discomfort if they add a wink.
The truth is painful.
Too painful to say
Much more painful to hold in my own way.
My way would be to grin and bear it
To pretend I sought to deliver and that I don't regret it.
This hurts my internal being so I'll protect myself
I won't say aloud but in the way I know best.
I do have a life and I do love to help.
But without a "thanks" or "I appreciate it" I begin to regret.
Regret the help I gave,
Regret the dedication,
Regret that I didn't say no,
Or make a stern impression.
Next time you can bet,
Every time in fact,
No is the answer you will get
When you ask me for help.

I'm So Happy

You think your life is hard;
by thinking this you make it harder.
You say you can only do "this";
"this" prevents you from going farther.
You repeat how "she did this and that" to you
Well she can stop now
because now you're doing it to yourself.
You pray to bear the pain
when you should pray for it to go away.
You complain because you don't have all that you want
You're silently forgetting what you've already got.
Do I have it all under lock and key?
No, of course not, but still look at me.
I'm thankful for what I have
I make my life satisfy me
I'm shooting for the stars and in ten years there's no telling
where I might be.
I'm So Happy!

Coming of Age

You think you know me because you made me.
At least you were there.
But I've grown up and there's a lot about
this woman you're unaware.
You never bothered to ask and I'm cool with that
But I hoped you were mature enough to judge based on fact.
Since you're not I'll tell you this,
I don't deal with people who keep up mess.
I love you dearly, that will never change but you have
brought your credibility with me down a long range.
I see what you think of me, it's not far from what I thought
It just hurts to see that it's true and obvious
without being sought.
Thanks for taking care of my self-esteem
and me for all those years.

As a Matter of Fact or Cut Like That

So you want to mind my business,
Be a part of my life?
Well, here's fair warning
I'm not afraid of what you bring: strife.
For strife was created to make me strong
And with God on my side I'll carry on.
As for you, believing everything you hear,
It would have hurt more if to me you were dear.
But I know your type, studied them well
And when you come around I'll just bail
I knew you had no faith in me.
I couldn't trust you, tossed two feet.
I just waited for the day the petty
you would meet the adult me.
You're mad at me? Who cares?
You're neither the man I married nor the
Man who died on the cross.
You're just the man who for over fifty years has been lost.

Avoid the Chore

My judgment is in your eyes,
Right next to the sparkle that holds the lies.
You're not slick nor are you clever
My true secrets will not be revealed; never.
Pick my brain see what you discover
You still won't know if I have an extra friend or lover.
Instead trust me and save your energy
Only believe what I allow you to see.
All else is assumed and purely circumstantial
If you must invest your time let it be on the actual.
Your stories will possess more merit.
Fewer people will waste time trying to dare it.
In the end you will have told the truth
Or at least had it as a foundation for your garbage juice.
Then you can hold your head although not very high
And you won't encounter having
to deny telling a bold faced lie
In other words, let me live my life and you live yours
Trying to do both is an unnecessary chore.

A Word to the Wise

You've achieved your goals, that's a beautiful thing
Your dream has come true just as you believed.
So what's next in line?
You certainly can't quit now.
What's your next move?
When will it be? And how?
Ponder for just a moment and search yourself
Isn't there more to life than the spotlight and wealth?
It's time you make a decision and make that first step.
As long as you follow Jesus you will be kept.

IV.

Occasionally we drift away...

An escape from reality is sometimes the cure for a long, tiring day. However, we can drift to the wrong place because we sin in thought, as well as word and deed. We can't stay too long because we are needed in reality.

Create a beautiful place in your mind that is sin-free. Stay away from dream homes and dream vacations because I have discovered that they can be a source of stress. Once we imagine we begin to ponder how to get there or the reasons we aren't there yet. Both equal stress. So be very careful of where your beautiful place will be. Once it's been created venture there for two or three minutes when your situations become overwhelming. Don't stay long, but occasionally drift away.

Blind Journey

A blind journey doesn't mean you can't see the road.
It means the road doesn't make sense.
I was constantly slowing down because I was driving too fast
But 35mph the stick would not pass.
I would see every relative I ever met
And those I didn't recognize were simply cousins I hadn't met yet.
Amazed that every traffic light was green just for me
Even the ones with a red tint let me be.
Blind journeys are dangerous to say the least
These blind journeys make room for the taunt of the beast.

Spotlight

This is where I need to be.
Up on stage for the entire world to see.
After all, God didn't make me up like this for nothing.
He created me to shine just like His many stars.
It's been a long time coming but I've found comfort, peace and fulfillment.
And it's right here before you, reciting what I've written.
I've always been so full of love for everyone I meet.
Sometimes the magic sparks at the very moment we greet.
Don't get me wrong; I'm not tooting my own horn
I'm sharing with you what my God has done.
He's allowed me an opportunity to fulfill my dreams.
In these days and times you don't know what that means.
It's so easy to mess up and step out of His will.
And unless you've been there you can't imagine how it feels.
But here I am so far from perfect and useless without Him
He preserved my gift and said share it with them.
Them is you and I'm so proud to share
The blessings of God and proof of how He cares.

V.

Through it all we must Speak Life...

Regardless of what you are experiencing right now you must speak life. That means speak the exact opposite of what you see.

If your child is disrespecting you when you talk to people say my child is very respectful. If the person sees your child and determines otherwise that's not your concern. You have already spoken life into that situation. Your words have power so your child will be respectful. (That was a reminder to me. I have a child beginning puberty so I have to be mindful of what I speak).

If your spouse is unfaithful and you must talk about it say that your spouse loves you and wants our marriage to be successful as much as I do. Then you work on making your marriage successful.

The key to speaking life is seeing God in all of your circumstances seek Him in the midst of it all. Once you find Him focus on Him and only Him. Doing this, first your heart will change and things won't hurt as much or affect you in the same manner. Next, your insight will change. You will no longer see the negative that you're facing; you will see the good God is creating in and through you. Your conversation will change. No longer will you bring down the mood of those you talk to. Your conversation will be upbeat and filled with expectancy. Finally, your circumstances will change because you will have begun to Speak Life!

The Real Thing

Some people wonder if there really is a God
If anyone asks, explaining is not very hard.
Tell them He is in things we can and cannot see.
Remind them of the sun, moon,
and stars and grass that's green.
If that doesn't work and they still have questions
Remind them how we scrape our knees and not get infections.
Ask them how the wind blows, no man can do that
And the way the rain falls,
and how the earth is round but the ground is flat.
We could go on naming all the amazing things God has done
Taking turns doing so would be fun.
But if your doubting friend still does not believe
Say to him, I am proof that God is real because
He lives inside of me!

Too Many Teachings

Others will tell you many different ways
To worship God and offer Him praise.
Some may tell you to stay on your knees
Others will say even that won't please.
The best way to know and be sure with no doubt
Is to seek God and follow Him as He points your way out.
He'll show you the right way and leave no room to question.
Remember, your right way was already predestined.

Anna Carson- The Seeker

You don't know me, asking why I'm sad.
I ain't sad, leave me alone, before you make me mad.
Sittin' there saying you're alive you should be glad.
Humph, like you know my existence, my day-to-day living.
Stop wasting my time with this stupid advice you're giving.
You're walking around whistling and singing church songs
But I've seen you with my own eyes doing wrong.
But telling me to smile and be content.
You can't guarantee where your own eternity will be spent
It doesn't really matter to me anyway.
Because when I die I'll just be dead
and won't have to face another day.
So don't bother telling me about some pie in the sky
I don't really care how you explain your reasons why.
You know what? Humor me.
Tell me about salvation, open my blinded eyes to see.

Ms. Melanie-The Sower

Anna, Anna how cross you are.
With that attitude you won't get far.
I know your situations may have been unusually bad
But that doesn't have to determine the type of life you have.
There's a way to be happy in all you do
It's when you give your cares away to Someone who's true.
Your only focus would have to be on Him, He's all that would matter
How to love Him, praise Him and get to know Him and His ways better.
It isn't very hard to do
Romans 10:9 says believe in your heart and confess with your mouth that Jesus died for you.
Will you still mess up? Yes. Guaranteed.
We all sin daily and fall short of the glory of God
But His grace and mercy keep us
Doesn't that seem pretty odd?
Well it's not, it all falls in line
Because when you confess in order to be saved you're saying my life is no longer mine.
If you can admit that you can't do it alone give your life to Christ and He will take it on.
You've already admitted that you're gonna mess up so He gives you grace and mercy so you won't give up.
If He's kept you thus far and you haven't come to Him
How much more will He be there for you when you are His?

Doubt and Reason

I've come to understand that it's not by my hand
Nor are my successes the work of any man.
If I'm honest with myself I must admit
It's Whose hands hold my destiny I have problems with.
I know they say God the Creator of all things
But how can He bless me as far as I am from wings?
I know He's real I don't doubt that
I even know His son Jesus is coming back.
My auntie always told me to have faith in the Lord.
But how do you know if you have faith
if in church you're always bored?
THE FRUITS OF YOUR LABOR
WILL ALWAYS SHINE THROUGH
AND THE WORD OF GOD IS ALWAYS TRUE.
IT'S A PROCESS WE ALL GO THROUGH AND GOD, BY
NAME, HAS CALLED YOU.
TALK TO HIM DAILY; CONSULT HIM ON ALL ISSUES
BE PREPARED TO PRAISE AND WORSHIP AND JUST IN
CASE BRING TISSUES.
FOR IF HE DIDN'T HOLD YOUR DESTINY
IN THE PALM OF HIS HAND
YOU WOULD HAVE BEEN DEVOURED
BY SATAN AND HIS CLAN.
INSTEAD YOU'RE HERE, CONFESS IT ALOUD:
I'M HERE TODAY BY GOD'S GRACE AND MERCY.
TODAY SATAN WILL NOT DETER ME.
AS I WALK TODAY THROUGH MY
PROCESS OF GROWTH
I'LL NOW BEGIN TO MAKE MENTAL NOTES
I'LL REMEMBER ALL THE THINGS GOD BRNGS ME
THROUGH TODAY
SO WHEN I GET HOME I CAN PRAISE, PRAISE, PRAISE.

Get Busy
(inspired by my Aunt Gail)

It's time to be about your Father's business
Sound like a cliché?
Well allow me to say it another way.
God is too good not to tell someone and not those who already know.
It's time to tell our stories to those who if the rapture came would not go.
We're sitting on power divinely given to us
We overcome by our testimony so it is a must.
What are you waiting for?
We've got to tell it all.
About all the times He held us when we were about to fall.
Don't hold it any more sinners' souls are crying
All we have to do is speak this out of our mouths.
God is good and He saves.
Read Romans 10:9 and discover His miraculous ways.

Make It Work

You're not alone or yet in distress
Satan just tries to make you feel like a mess.
But the devil is a liar the Word says so
And it's up to you to tell the devil no.
It's okay to mourn, for Jesus did so for us
To say it's not okay would be totally unjust.
Just remember Whose you are
On that alone you will go far.
There's no limit to the goals you can achieve
It's all in you but first you must believe.
Once you believe take it out of your hands
Put it in the hands of the Man who designed the Plan.

Who Are You?

Let me talk to you sister.
Do you know who you are?
You're beauty, inspiration, a rock, and shining star.
You hold your man up when he's weary and worn
You prepare your children with love each and every morn.
Listen to me sister, know who you are.
You're wanted, needed, destined to go far.
Don't get caught up in the right now
Press through with the determination to make it somehow.
Many are depending on you to finish this race.
As we celebrate at the finish line, sister my sister
I want to look over and see your face.

Love Anew

You may feel like you're doing it alone
At times things pile up one after the other and make you feel
all hope is gone.
But on this day I'd like to encourage you
I'd like to share with you a Word that is always true:
God won't put more on you than you can bear
So whatever you're going through don't view it as unfair.
God saw strength enough in you to carry this load.
He saw faith enough to let you go down this road.
His grace and mercy have kept you thus far that's why you
haven't lost your mind.
A God who knows all you've done and
continues to keep you is so kind.
While you go through,
turn to God and tell Him your thoughts
Let Him share His kindness with you and help you find peace
with your faults.
Let Him love on you as only He can
He will please you far better than any man.
He won't forget your birthday or any special events.
He'll assure all time spent with Him will be time well spent.
So on this day I offer to you
An encouragement to renew your relationship with God, a
love that's pure.

Keep the Faith

Don't lose hope, the battle is not done
You can't forget that the battle's already won.
Jesus has defeated your enemy for sure.
All you have to do is press and endure.

Looking Upon (dedicated to Tony)

I look into your eyes and see success
I pray daily that you'll receive the best
I love you dearly and I say aloud
You, my love, have made me proud!

Ponder Life (dedicated to Jaylin)

Think on what life is and what life you see.
Say to yourself what can my life really be.
Anything you want, no holds barred
Just remember your Source and keep Him in charge.
Ponder life and all that's in store
As long as you're truly serving God there's no sin in wanting more.

Never Alone

I know sometimes we feel alone just like no one cares,
But this is to let you know you're
always in my thoughts and prayers.
This walk gets hard at times and we
sometimes want to give up
That's when we have to remember the good things
that happen are blessings not luck.
Hold on some more
And whenever you need support,
call on the sisters and we'll come forth.
We'll hold you up not tear you down
Because when we're in heaven praising we want you to be
around.

The Little Things

If making a dream come true were easy
there would be no reason to dream.
If everything were music to our ears
there would be no reason to sing.
If heaven were on earth there would be no goal.
Without the goal there'd be no reason to save our souls.
The little things lead to bigger things
and are our ultimate purpose.
Appreciate the little things so you can enjoy the others.

Sunset Rivers

Looking at the sunrise new and warm
Brings hopes of new beginnings and comfort of past mistakes gone on.
As darkness breaks with the light of day
Your strength is in knowing you can now see your way.
Strive to make your way while your path is clear.
Work knowing that night is drawing near.
When sunset approaches and the light begins to dim
Remember to look to the heavens and acknowledge Him
For in the sunset comfortable and warm
Is the beauty of all great things passed on.
Beauty is in the eye of the beholder this is true
And behold all the great beauty that lies in you.

In Prayer

Where am I strong despite my body's aches and pains?
Where am I knowledgeable when in a new place?
Where is there peace in the midst of my chaos?
Where can I be found safe and secure while I am lost?
Where are the answers to the questions that plague us?
Where is the cure to the flesh's lust?
Where is this place?
To know is a must.
All of these things are found in a place for the prepared.
All is found in the secret place called prayer.

Fire and Desire

The feeling inside is undeniably fresh and new every time.
Coming in contact with God
does much more than blow your mind.
It can kill the things that are not of Him
But only if your heart is receiving and sincere.
With an open heart you can be filled with a fire
And as the fire shimmers, it fuels your heart's desire.
Cause and effect?
Feed the fire and desire what you elect.
God gives us choices and a means to achieve.
But again, you must feed your fire and truly believe.

Create a Praise

Our hearts are broken in so many ways,
It's not always because some man has left us in a daze.
True that happens and it hurts down deep.
But so many other things cause women of character to weep.
Like when a child is hurting, and not just your own
We feel their pain as if they were ours, blood born.
The hurt of our sisters who are going through
more than we do.
We suffer as if it were happening to us, too.
Our families and their issues,
and everyone seems to have some,
Lay on our shoulders as we ponder solutions
to help them overcome.
As saved, sanctified women of character
there's something we must learn to do.
That's praise and worship God
no matter what we're going through.
I know it's not easy considering all we're faced with
But He's so worthy the sacrifice is worth it.
I've learned a little something
and it helps me make it through.
For those of you who may be broken,
I'd like to share it with you.
When my heart is heavy and tears are near
I lift my eyes unto the hills.
I say hallelujah, at first, just the word
Because that is the highest praise
no matter what you've heard.
The more I say it and think of His goodness
My praise elevates and becomes spirit moving.

When praises go up blessings come down
And that alone can remove a frown
But what really happens in the midst of your praise.
Is Daddy comes down and adjusts some things.
He makes a way out of no way,
And opens doors that were closed
He puts His arms around His daughters
And until they're better He holds.
He heals all that ails you, restores your joy
and renews your strength.
He reminds you that He's the weapon you're fighting with.
He forgives all you ask Him to
And with His mercy gives you a chance, brand new.
So that's how I praise in the midst of a circumstance.
Beginning with a simple word, hallelujah,
I get another chance.
Another chance to praise Him with song and dance.
Another chance to serve Him like I never have.
Sisters I beg you, follow suit
Create a way to stir up your praise
when you're going through.
Discover the many blessings and the many miracles
God has stored up just for you.

Hearts of Gold

The heart of you who take us in
Giving us hope that somehow we'll win.
Is larger than most and filled with something special.
That something special is care, concern, and love on an un-
natural level.
God made you separate from all the rest
And I believe He'll bless you best.
So in your obedience remember God sees what you've done
And know that you know your best is yet to come.

Talent Breathes Deeply

If talent were a look here's what you'd see
Hair so normal it's strange and eyes as deep as the sea.
Glance at talent and you'd have to look again
Because in talent you'll see a passion to win.
Look closely and you'll see goals and ideas intertwined.
Although you could never truly interpret talent's mind.
For as soon as you think you've got it pegged,
You'll begin to feel you've been misled.
However, don't fret because talent is not cold.
In fact, he's loving and quite bold.
Doing all he can to make you happy is his goal.
So embrace any talent that you see
It was created to enthrall you and me.

Thank You

Another day given, filled with mercies everlasting
A chance to love God more, a day to stop taking chances.
Commitment to be all that I can be
Promises to keep growing and adhere to what I see.
I thank you God for showing me the way
I thank you God for keeping me so I can stay.
Stay strong in Your will and ever in Your word,
Stay willing to obey all from You that I've heard.
Thank You for being a loving God
Thank You for being my God.
Thank You for Your mercies and grace.
Thank You for blessing me with
the honor of running this race.

More than Thank You

God gives us what we can handle, no more no less.
Some of what He gives us is solely a test.
Not a blessing per say because He intends for us to have more
So what He gives us is an opportunity for gratitude to show.
But you're still where you were as obedient as you are.
But aside from the thanks you say aloud,
how thankful are you in your heart?
Do you really appreciate the things you've been given?
Or are you anxious to change the way you're living?
There's nothing wrong with being innovative
and wanting better
But unless you're willing to accept what you have you're
successfully stagnating your blessing.
So be thankful in your heart not just in words and talk.
That way your blessings will manifest in your life and prosper
your walk.

One Moment

I always imagine what I'd say in my one moment to shine
With pen in hand I search my mind.
The Truth, just as it is written in the Holy Word
But that moment may not last long enough to kill every myth
you've heard.
My being here is a living, breathing testimony
But this moment isn't long enough to share my story.
Very briefly, it involves bullets,
promiscuity, sickness and stress
I'm sure that if you turned the pages of your life
you'd find no less.
So what are you trying to say sister, why are you here?
Your moment is almost up the end is near.
That's it my brother, you hit it on the head.
The end is near; pretty soon we'll all be dead.
I'm here to say salvation is real
I'll be your personal witness
God sent His Son, the only Chosen One,
He did die and rise again.
Because of Him we can live long after we die
You could argue that point but why?
A life in salvation, true salvation, is one of peace and joy.
He also offers abundance and a whole lot more.
So why dispute the color of His skin
When His Spirit is what gives us power within.
My moment is ending and as it winds down
I encourage you all to claim your crown.
It isn't difficult, don't listen to man.
All that's required are that you admit you can't fix yourself
and believe God can.

I encourage you today to seek God for yourself
Not for any person or for wealth.
People always want a hookup and it makes no sense.
Your best bet is to hook up with the One who created all this.
Imagine being personally connected to the One who made the trees, none of which are the same.
Connected to the One who before
He said let there be light, knew your name.
My moment is gone but God lives on.
Seek Him and you will find Him, His Spirit and His Son.
Thanks for my moment.

Printed in the United States
75736LV00006B/183